Puttering with Paper

by A. Harris Stone
and Bertram M. Siegel

ILLUSTRATED BY PETER P. PLASENCIA

PRENTICE-HALL, INC., ENGLEWOOD CLIFFS, N. J.

For Martin, Jimmy,
Robin, and Mandy

Puttering with Paper by A. Harris Stone and Bertram M. Siegel

© 1968 by A. Harris Stone and Bertram M. Siegel

Library of Congress Catalog Card Number: 68-17528
Printed in the United States of America   J

Prentice-Hall International, Inc., London
Prentice-Hall of Australia, Pty. Ltd., Sydney
Prentice-Hall of Canada, Ltd., Toronto
Prentice-Hall of India Private Ltd., New Delhi
Prentice-Hall of Japan, Inc., Tokyo

CONTENTS

INTRODUCTION

Throughout the course of history, progress in science has been the product of men's minds. More than two thousand years ago, basic ideas of the atomic structure of matter were discussed in Greece by Democritus. As time went on, men developed ideas about what caused the "happenings" in the universe. In most cases, an individual's idea did not stand the test of time and was forgotten. However, many great contributions to the world of science were made by the men whose ideas were remembered. These men, whom we now call great scientists, had as a unique characteristic the ability to think for themselves. Most important, they were individuals who were not afraid to experiment and to believe the things they saw. They asked many questions—

WHAT HAPPENED?
HOW DID IT HAPPEN?
WHAT MADE IT HAPPEN?

In reading this book you will have an opportunity to experiment as scientists have throughout history. To do this, you must be willing to experiment without much knowledge about the problem and to experiment in ways not described in this book. In fact, you must seek answers to the questions asked here in the best ways you can. Do not be afraid to try anything that seems sensible to you. The worst thing that can happen to any experiment is that it will fail—and failure is a scientist's constant companion.

Most of the experiments in this book have a scientist's name as a title, in honor of the person who developed many of the ideas presented by the experiment. One of the reasons they are titled this way is to help you find out more about the topic being studied. For example, as you perform the experiments in the section entitled "Sir Robert Hooke," you will be asking many of the same questions the great scientist Robert Hooke asked when he was searching for ideas about *why* and *how* objects stretch. If you need more information about the ideas you are studying, you can look up the work of Sir Robert Hooke.

When you turn this page, you will enter the experimental world of some of history's greatest scientists. Don't be afraid to experiment in your own way.

BENJAMIN FRANKLIN

What happens to small scraps of paper when a rubber comb that has been rubbed on wool, silk, or fur is brought close to them?

Will a cylinder of rolled paper rubbed on the same materials have the same effect on the scraps as the comb did? How about a plastic pen?

What happens to two strips of paper when they are "stroked" many times by the thumb and forefinger? Does it matter what kind of paper is used? Does it matter if this is done on a humid day or a dry day?

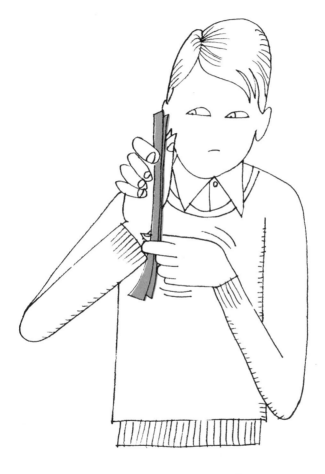

Do the length and width of the strips make any difference? What happens if you blow on strips that have been rubbed? On strips that have not been rubbed?

What happens to two narrow strips of aluminum foil that have been hung from a piece of wire when a "charged" comb is brought close to them? What happens when the comb touches them?

What happens to the strips if you touch the wire with your finger after the comb touches the wire?

When aluminum foil hung from wire is placed in a glass container, it is called an *electroscope* and can be used to detect electric charges.

These experiments are based on a phenomenon called *static electricity*. The effects that you have observed are common to many objects and are a result of the energy produced when objects are rubbed with certain materials. The Greeks knew about static electricity more than two thousand years ago. They observed that a material which we call *amber* and they called "elektron" would attract bits of other materials if the amber was first rubbed on animal fur. The English scientist William Gilbert was the first to call this attracting force "electricity," from the Greek word "elektron." He also found that some materials other than amber showed this behavior when they were rubbed. The French scientist Charles de Cisterney discovered that when two rods of the same material were rubbed, they would repel each other and that two different rods, when rubbed, would attract each other.

As clouds move through the atmosphere they become charged with electricity in much the same way as a rod does when it is rubbed with a piece of fur. A *large collection of electrons may be built up on the cloud*. Sometimes this collection of electrons, called the charge, becomes so large that the cloud discharges them. The electron discharge is in the form of a gigantic group of electrons jumping from cloud to cloud or from the cloud to the earth. When this jump occurs, it is visible as lightning and is accompanied by the crashing sound called thunder.

The investigator who discovered that lightning was static electricity was Benjamin Franklin. His famous kite experiment established him as one of the first American scientists and eventually gained worldwide prestige for the then infant United States.

LEONARDO DA VINCI

Can a piece of paper be flown if it is folded as shown in the illustration below? Does the size of the sheet of paper used to make the airplane have any effect on the distance it flies?

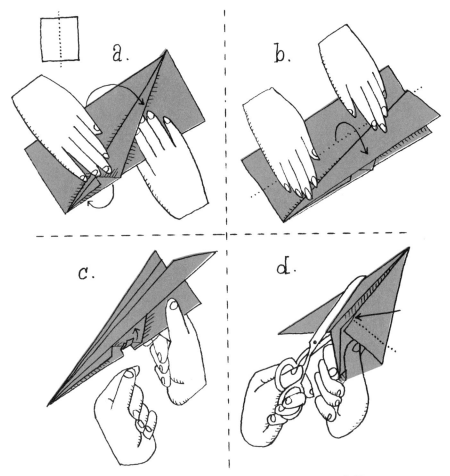

Does the kind of paper used make any difference in the ability of the plane to fly?

14

What is the effect on the flight of the plane if its "flaps" are folded up? Does the size of the flaps make any difference in the plane's flight? What happens to the flight of the plane if the flaps are turned down?

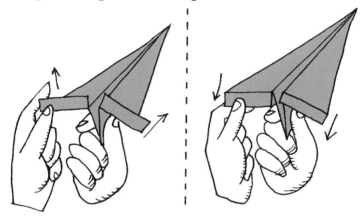

Is it important that the flaps be of equal size? Does the shape of the flaps make any difference?

What is the effect on the flight if only one flap is up? Only one is down? If one flap is up and one is down?

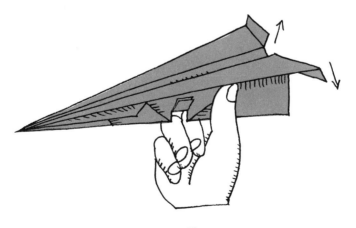

What is the effect on the distance of the plane's flight if a paper clip is attached to the body of the plane? Is this effect doubled if two paper clips are used? Tripled if three are used?

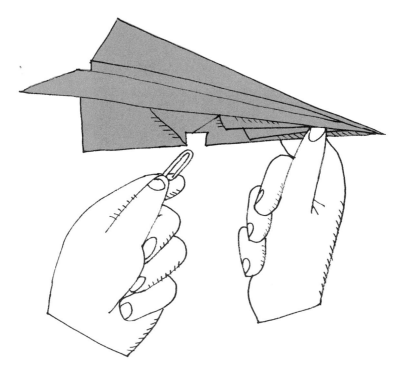

Is the position of the paper clip on the plane's body important? What other factors affect the distance of the plane's flight?

One of the most brilliant minds in the history of man was the Italian scientist, Leonardo da Vinci. Hundreds of years before the space age, he designed and built models of airplanes—none of which could "fly." Not

16

until 1903 and the Wright brothers would man fly in a craft that was heavier than air. Some of the problems that both Da Vinci and the Wright brothers faced were the design of wings, flaps and tails of airplanes. What problem was Da Vinci unable to solve, which, when solved by the Wright brothers, enabled them to be successful?

The history of mankind and of science is filled with examples of problems like the one shared by Leonardo, Orville and Wilbur—the ideas came long before the inventions that made them possible. A present-day example of this is that although men have thought of flights to the moon for thousands of years such thoughts were fantasy until very recently.

Today there are many creative people who are thinking of new ideas. These new ideas are the basis for the inventions and technology of tomorrow. In trying to make these ideas workable, scientists invent and develop the practical "things" of tomorrow. One of the almost unbelievable new ideas which scientists are now trying to make workable is undersea farming. Man has always taken a small amount of food from the sea, but with the tremendous need to feed the world's constantly increasing population, scientists are now trying to make the sea a major source of food. What problems are they facing? What are some of the possible solutions to these problems? Even though hundreds of scientists are working to solve these problems, very little is known about what will make ocean farming possible. The information that is needed to solve this problem will come from those people who become interested in the problem—perhaps you.

THOMAS YOUNG

What happens when a piece of paper that has been folded many times is struck sharply? Does the kind of paper make any difference? Does it matter how the paper is held?

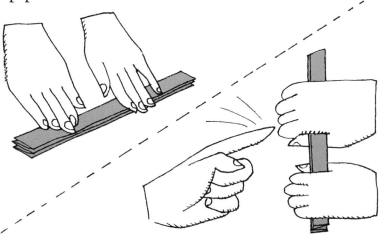

Try striking a pencil instead of the folded paper. Does paper break more easily than wood?

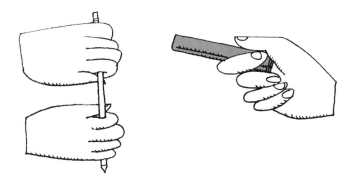

What happens if many paper strips are struck sharply instead of the folded piece of paper? How many strips must be used if a different effect is to be produced? Does the kind of paper make a difference? Does it matter if the paper is wet? Does it matter if the folded paper is twisted?

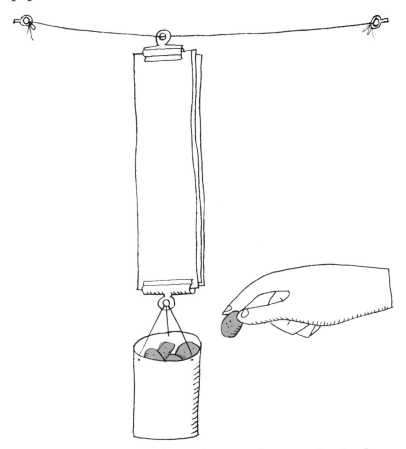

Will the same number of strips that can be broken with a sharp blow break if a large amount of weight is slowly hung on them?

What would happen to a steel bar if two men pulled on it in opposite directions? Does the thickness of the bar make any difference? What happens to a strip of paper that is pulled in opposite directions? Does the thickness or number of strips make any difference? Does twisting the paper or strips have any effect?

Does the kind of paper make any difference?

The amount of force needed to pull a strip of paper apart can be measured by adding weights to the free end of a strip of paper attached to a support.

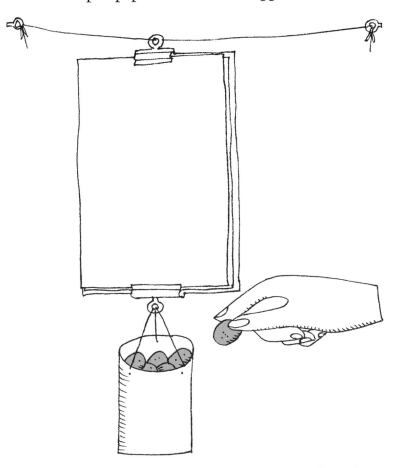

Does a strip of paper that is twice the width of another strip break when the same amount of weight is added to both? What factors can be shown to affect the amount of weight required to break a strip of paper?

Does breaking a piece of paper depend on the position in which it is held? What happens when you push with your finger on a long strip of paper that has been stretched tightly and secured at both ends? Is any difference felt when a shorter piece of paper of the same width and thickness is used?

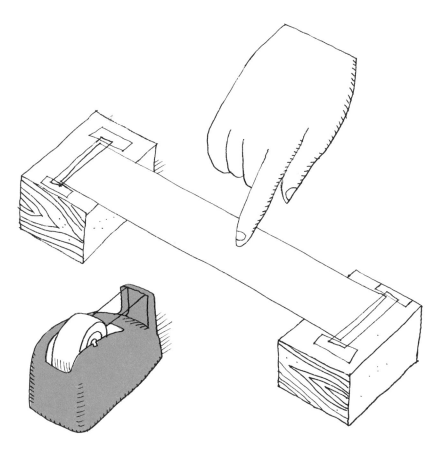

Does wetting the paper have any effect?

The strength of materials is of great importance to scientists, inventors, manufacturers, architects, builders, in fact, anyone who has anything to do with materials. Imagine what would happen if a bridge were built of candy canes and chewing gum instead of girders and rivets!

Some materials are more useful than others for such projects as bridge-building because of their strength. For example, steel is preferred to wood when the construction of a bridge or tall office building is being considered. The strength of materials is often compared on the basis of each material's *tensile* value. The *tensile strength* of a material is determined by the amount of force required to pull it apart.

In order to judge the relative strength of different materials, a scientist named Thomas Young devised a system to compare tensile strengths of various materials. In this system, the tensile value calculated for each material is compared to that of a particular material chosen to serve as a standard. *Young's modulus*, as this comparison is called, is extremely useful to engineers and scientists when they are choosing materials to do special jobs.

Which of the following materials has the greatest tensile strength? The least? Aluminum; Silly Putty; wood; copper; paper.

EVANGELISTA TORRICELLI

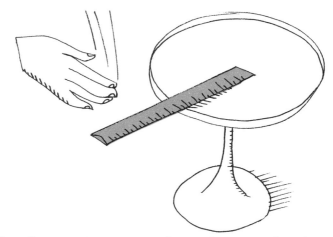

What happens to a wooden ruler or other board when it is placed so that part of it extends over the edge of a table and the extended end is struck sharply?

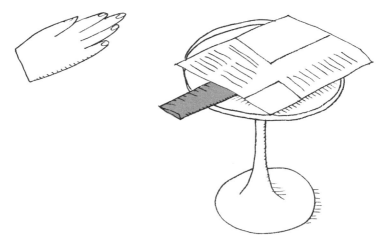

What happens to the same ruler after it has been covered with newspaper and the extended end is struck sharply?

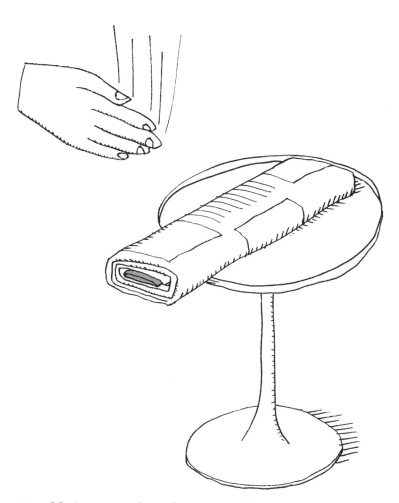

Would the same thing happen if the experiment were to be repeated with the newspaper folded as much as possible?

What would be the effect on a flowerpot if it were used in place of the newspaper? Would you believe this should be done out of doors?

What happens when a glass half-full of water is covered with an index card and turned upside down? Does it matter how much water is in the glass?

Do this over a sink or wear rubbers!

Is the air pressure in the half-full glass the same as the air pressure outside of the glass? Does the air pressure in the glass change when the card is placed on top of it? Does it change when the glass is turned over? What holds the card on the glass?

CAREFUL—THIS IS NOT AS OBVIOUS AS IT SEEMS!!

It was not until Torricelli invented the *barometer* in 1643 that problems concerning air weight and pressure could be studied. The effects of air pressure have always been of great interest to scientists because air pressure is common to all experiments and experimenters, but may vary from place to place and from time to time.

A large number of experiments and questions may be based on air pressure and air weight. For example, the American Indians knew that it takes longer for water to boil on a mountaintop that it does in a valley. Even though the Indians had no scientific reasons to explain why this happened, they were able to use this knowledge.

Air pressure is important in the operation of many objects we use every day, though we do not often realize it. For example, the operation of pressure cookers, refrigerator cooling systems, fireplace chimneys and heating systems are all dependent on air pressure. How is air pressure connected with each one of these?

GALILEO GALILEI

Galileo Galilei discovered that all things fall at the same rate. Decide if Galileo was right after doing this experiment.

Sharply strike the prop that holds up the inclined plane.

What happens to the marble that is resting on the small hole in the rigid cardboard plane? Does it make a difference if the cup is attached to the plane?

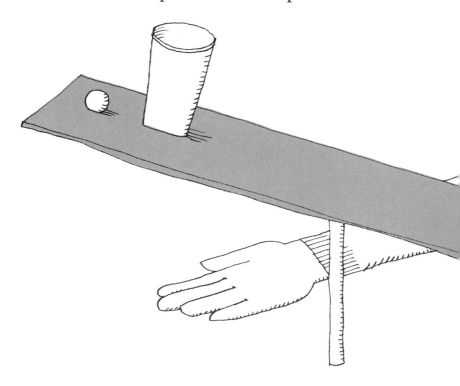

Does it make any difference where the prop that holds up the plane is placed? Does it matter how hard or in what direction you strike the prop?

STICK WITH THIS ONE—IT'S DIFFICULT!

Does the distance of the cup from the end of the plane have any effect on the outcome of the experiment? Does it matter how close the marble is to the cup?

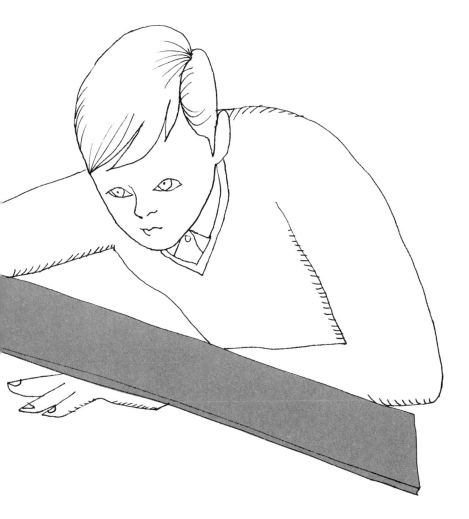

Which of the following hits the floor first when dropped from the same height: a flat piece of paper, an equal size sheet of paper folded, or an equal size piece of paper rolled into a ball?

Is it important to use the same kind of paper?
What would happen if the paper were wet?

A story is told of how Galileo Galilei first proved that regardless of their weight, all things fall at the same rate. Supposedly, he dropped two objects of different weights from the top of the Leaning Tower of Pisa. This story may not be true, but your experimentation has given you evidence to decide upon the truth of the theory. If your decision disagrees with that of the great scientist, can you explain why?

Another scientist who worked on the problem of falling objects and gravity was Sir Isaac Newton. He, too, was able to calculate the speed at which objects fell. By comparing his calculations with those made by Galileo, Newton was able to show that Galileo's results were "correct." Although Newton and Galileo lived at different times, the work of one scientist was built upon the work of the other just as your work is built on both of theirs. This was what Newton meant when he said, "If I have seen further, it is because I have stood on the shoulders of giants."

SIR ISAAC NEWTON

What happens when a weight which is suspended by a strip of paper is pulled hard but slowly by another piece of paper that is attached to it? What happens if it is pulled rapidly?

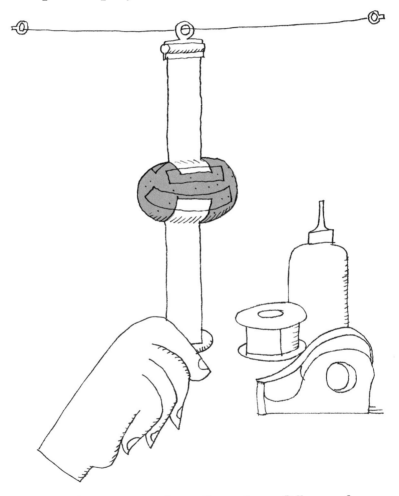

Does the amount of weight make a difference?

Is it important to use the same kind of paper through-out both experiments?

What would happen if waxed paper were used above the weight in each trial and tissue paper were used below the weight? If tissue paper were used above the weight and waxed paper below?

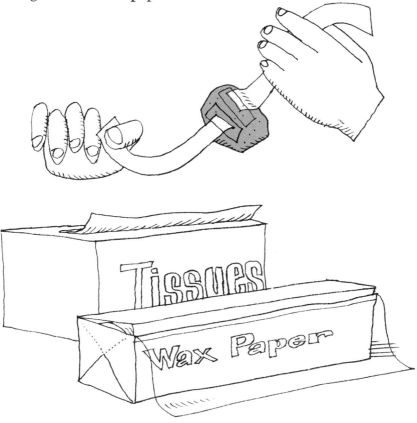

What would be the effect on each trial if the paper strips supporting the weights were soaked in water or alcohol before attaching the weights?

If a sheet of paper is stretched over a frame, and a heavy metal ball is placed gently in the center, what will be the effect? If the ball is dropped on the paper?

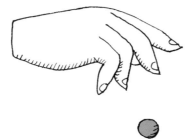

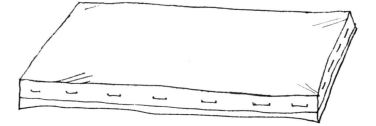

Does it matter how high above the paper the ball is held when it is dropped? Does the kind of paper make any difference?

After doing these experiments, what evidence can be found to support Sir Isaac Newton's statement that ". . . a body at rest tends to stay at rest and a body in motion tends to stay in motion unless acted upon by an outside force"?

He was talking about forms of *inertia,* or resistance to change. An object that is at rest is said to have the property of *inertia of rest* and an object that is moving is said to have the property of *inertia of motion.* On the basis of these experiments, what can be done to change the kind of inertia that an object has? For example, when a car traveling at 70 miles per hour smashes into a brick wall something happens to both the car and the wall. Does the inertia of the car change? The inertia of the wall? What happens when an "irresistible force" meets an "immovable object"? Is there such a thing as an "irresistible force" or an "immovable object"?

In the last experiment, the ball that was dropped on the paper had a different kind of inertia than the ball that was placed gently on the paper. In both cases, the inertia of the paper did not change. If the paper is wet, what happens to its inertia?

WHO?

What happens to a wet piece of paper when it is placed against the wall? Does the paper change position if it is allowed to dry while on the wall? Does it matter if the paper is wet with a liquid other than water?

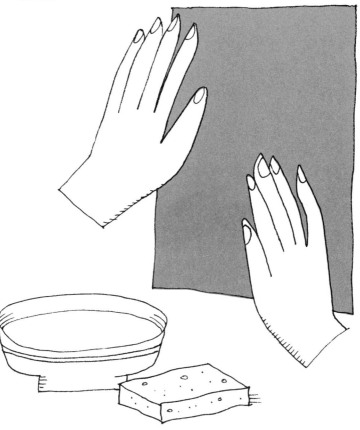

Do all kinds of paper *adhere* to walls when they are wet? Will strips of paper *adhere* to each other if they are not wet?

Is it more difficult to pull a piece of wet paper off a wall than it is to pull a piece of cellophane tape off the same wall? What happens when two pieces of cellophane tape are placed sticky sides together? Can they be pulled apart? Is it more difficult to pull these apart than to pull tape off the top of a kitchen counter?

Do two pieces of tape with sticky sides together *cohere* or *adhere*?

Can the amount of cohesion or adhesion between two sticking objects be measured? When two circles of paper are attached to each other with water how many pins or paper clips must be added to the cup that is attached to the bottom circle in order to pull them apart? How much weight is needed to separate the circles when petroleum jelly or salad oil is used instead of water to attach the circles to each other?

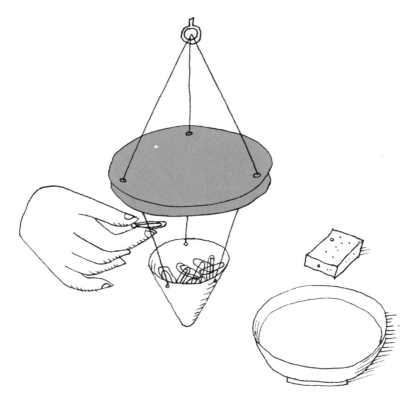

Does the size of the paper circles have any effect on the amount of weight needed to separate them? Does the kind of paper have any effect?

WHO was the first man to develop ideas about adhesion? WHEN was the idea developed and WHAT was the original idea?

Why is a block of wood one piece rather than sawdust or many pieces? What holds the block of wood together? All materials that are in one piece stay in one piece unless they are acted upon by some outside force. The "thing" that keeps a material together is the attractive force that the particles of the object have for each other. Remember how difficult it was to pull apart two pieces of tape that had been placed sticky side together? Is it easier to pull off a piece of tape that has been stuck to something else? The amount of difficulty in separating the tape-to-tape as compared to the tape-to-something-else is an indication of the difference between cohesive forces and adhesive forces.

Cohesive forces are those between particles of the same material and adhesive forces are the forces between different kinds of particles. A block of wood is held in one piece by the cohesive forces of all of its particles. A comparison between the strengths of adhesive and cohesive forces can be made by testing the resistance that a block of wood offers to being pulled apart as compared to the resistance offered by an equal size block made from sawdust glued together.

Substances that are used to hold different things together are called adhesive materials or "glues." The term "glue" as used here is a general term. All glues work on specific kinds of materials. For example, it would be very difficult to hold two wires together with a glue made of flour and water. It would be equally difficult to "glue" two pieces of wood together with solder.

WHAT?

What happens when one end of a strip of paper toweling is placed in a glass of water and the other end is placed in an empty glass?
BE PATIENT WHEN DOING THIS EXPERIMENT!

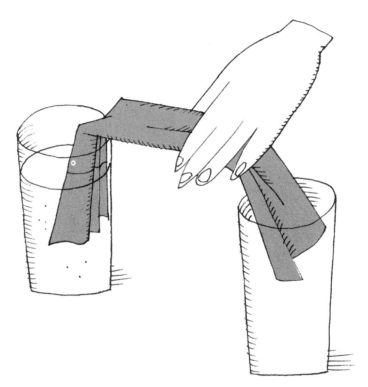

Does it matter if the empty glass is higher or lower than the full glass?
Will this experiment work with a piece of cloth instead of paper? Does the width of the paper make any difference?

What happens when one end of a long strip of paper toweling is hung in a glass containing a solution of three different food colorings in water?

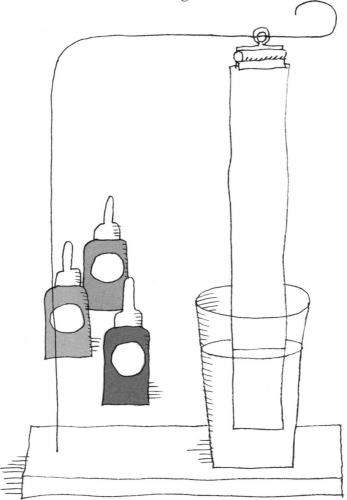

Does the length, width, or kind of paper have any effect on what occurs?

What is the effect of the temperature of liquids on their ability to be absorbed? What happens if one end of a strip of napkin is placed in a cup of very hot water and the other end is placed in a cup containing the same amount of very cold water?

Does adding vegetable coloring to the water help in making observations?

Do the length and width or kind of paper have any effect on the experiment?

WHAT was the last idea of capillarity to be discovered and WHO discovered it? WHEN was this done?

The movement of water from place to place within some materials is due to an unusual phenomenon called *capillary action*. The water appears to move within substances (like paper) through tube-like spaces between the particles that make up the substance. What part do adhesion and cohesion play in capillary action?

Capillary action has been known to man for hundreds of years and like so many other great discoveries, the identity of the scientist who first observed this phenomenon has been lost to the world. Our present knowledge is due to the work of many scientists, including the French scientist LaPlace and the American Thomas Young.

Sap, water, and dissolved materials move upward through trees by capillary action. Within the human body are very important structures called *capillaries*. These tiny tubes carry blood and liquids from place to place and are essential for normal body functions.

WHEN?

What is the effect on a strip of paper that is held tightly between the thumbs when a strong stream of air is blown on it? What happens if the paper is not held between the thumbs when the air is blown on it?

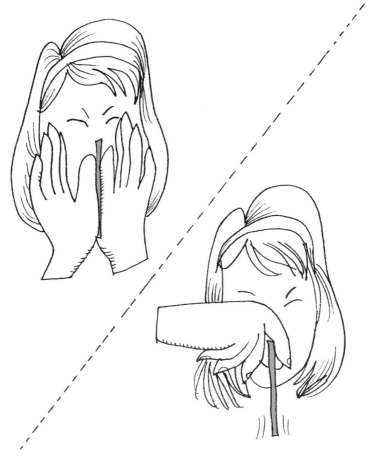

How does the thickness of the paper "reed" effect the *pitch* of the sound? Does blowing harder change the *amplitude* of the sound?

44

What can be heard when a waxed paper covered comb is placed against the lips of a person who is humming? Will the same sound be produced if the waxed paper is soaked in water before it is used?

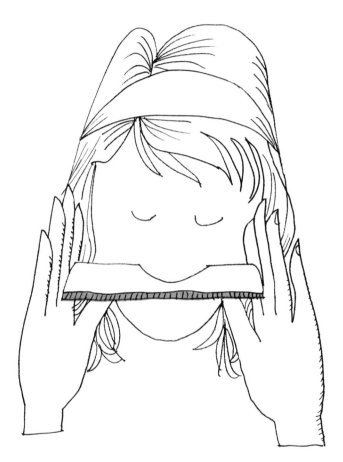

Do the *vibrations* change if tissue paper is used instead of waxed paper?

The effect of vibrating air in a tube can be studied by building a simple version of the musical instrument called a "bongo drum." A bongo drum can be made by stretching and securing paper tightly across a can that has been opened at both ends. Rubber bands will help. Two different-size cans attached together make a set of "bongos."

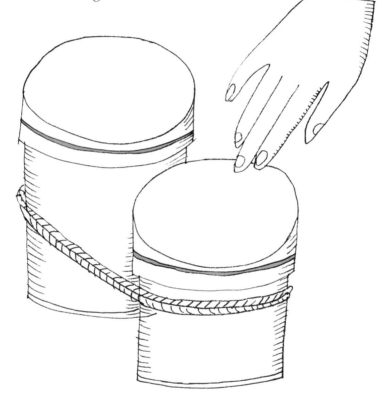

What are the differences in the sounds produced by bongos that have different diameters and lengths?

What is the effect on the sound if different kinds of paper are used?

WHEN were the first ideas about sounds developed, WHO developed them and WHAT were they?

In our modern world it is almost impossible to spend as little as five minutes without hearing any sound. Even if a person was alone in a desert, sounds produced by the forces of nature would be heard constantly. The moving air or *wind* would create sound as it passed through the sagebrush and other desert plants.

Regardless of where a person is on the earth, he will find sounds that are characteristic of that geographical area. The wind whispering in the pines, the gentle breezes that blow across the meadows, and the rushing currents of air that sweep down mountainsides are all products of nature's "sound factory."

The human body is very much dependent upon recognizing kinds of sounds and the amplitudes of sounds for safety and direction. The constant pounding of the surf, the roar of a waterfall, and the babbling of a brook tell man that he is nearing water long before the water is visible. The sound of an automobile horn, the shot of a gun or the roar of a railroad train all cause a reaction that produces in man an awareness of the possibility of nearby danger.

JEAN PIAGET

Is it possible to measure the weight of a small piece of paper? By building the apparatus illustrated below, it will be possible to make very accurate weight measurements.

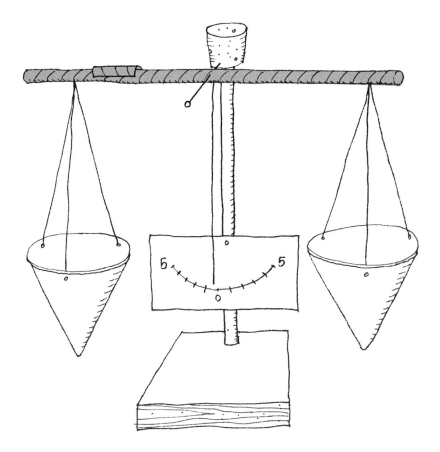

Of what value is the small section of straw which slides along the main straw?

What is the effect on the weight of a piece of paper when it is crumpled into a small ball or rolled into a tight cylinder? By placing the paper in one cup and adding small pins to the other until a balance is reached, the weight of paper in "pin units" can be found.

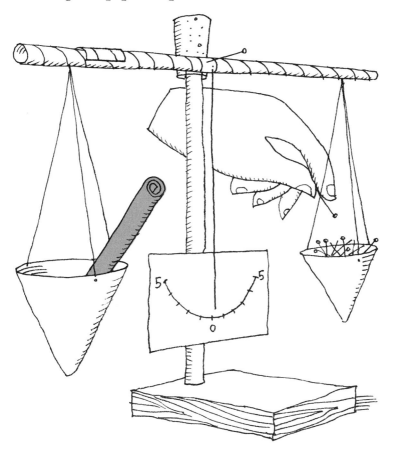

What happens to the weight of the paper if it is torn into many pieces and all of the pieces are weighed together?

Does dropping a piece of paper into water change the total weight of the paper when it is weighed? Does the paper weigh the same after it has dried out as it did before it was weighed? How can you be sure the paper is as dry as it was before?

Do different kinds of paper absorb different amounts of water? Is it important to use the same size pieces of paper? Does the kind of liquid absorbed by the paper, alcohol, for example, have any effect on the total weight?

Not all scientists study materials or the action of materials with each other. Some scientists are more concerned with *how* people learn what they know than with the things they know about.

Jean Piaget of Switzerland is a living scientist who has spent most of his life trying to discover how people learn things such as the *conservation of mass*.

He has found that most people are able to understand that even though the shape of a substance may be changed, the amount of material does not change. According to Dr. Piaget, most people are able to understand "conservation" by the time they are twelve years old.

Being able to learn about things does not only depend on age. Other factors are equally important, including the ability to read, count, and think about things that have not been seen or handled. For example, although no one has ever seen atoms, we are able to think about them and to consider them real. The ability to think about things such as atoms is called the ability to think *abstractly* and is a measure of basic intelligence.

Think back to the experiments with the weight of paper. Did the amount of space that the paper took up change when the shape of the paper changed?

ENGINEERS

What is the effect on a sheet of paper that has been rolled into the shape of a cylinder as books are gently placed on top of it one at a time? Does the size of the cylinder make any difference?

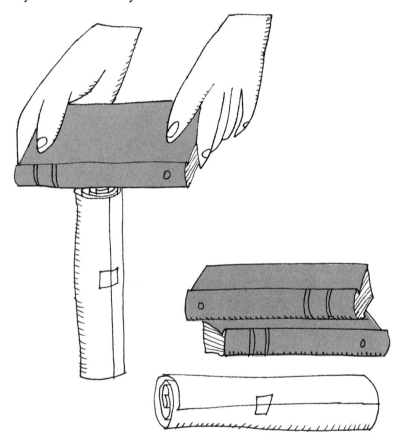

Is there any difference if two or more pieces of paper are used to make the cylinder?

Does the kind of paper used make any difference?

Will a piece of paper folded into a rectangle support the same number of books as a cylinder will?

Which geometric shape will support the most books?

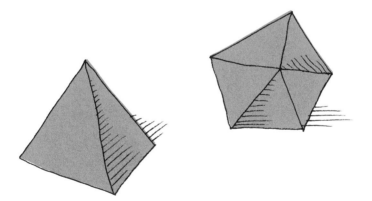

Does the size and weight of the books make any difference?

Will the effect be the same if a large number of thin sheets are used instead of a few sheets of thicker paper?

What happens to paper crumpled into the shape of a ball as books are placed upon it one at a time? Does the "ball" flatten out as much with the second book as it did with the first? With the third as it did with the second?

Does it matter how tightly you crumple the paper when you form the ball?

Is there any difference if four paper balls are used, one in each corner of the book?

Engineers are special kinds of scientists who work with materials as well as ideas. They are concerned with questions of what materials are, how they behave and how they can be best used. One of their important problems is deciding how strong a material is.

Although tensile strength is one important factor in selecting materials for building things, another equally important factor is the material's *compressional strength.* Based on these experiments, it seems that the force required to compress a material can vary. The shape into which a material is formed is an important factor in its ability to resist being compressed.

Will a steel cylinder support more books than a paper one? Does this depend on the kind of paper? In Japan, paper is used to build houses. Would such houses support as much snow on their roofs as houses made of wood?

One way to compare the compressional strength of shapes and kinds of materials is to experiment with eggs.

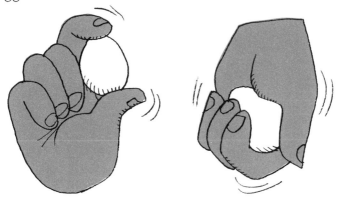

What happens if compressional strength is applied to the ends of an egg? To the sides of an egg?

SIR ROBERT HOOKE

What happens when a flat piece of paper which has been cut into a "spiral" is pulled down and then let go?

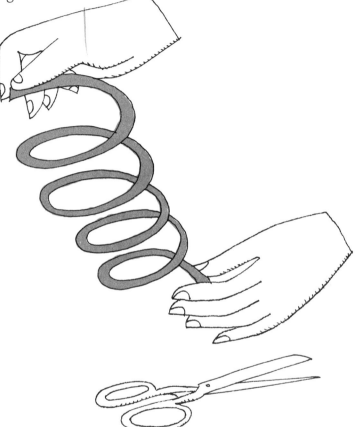

Is there any limit to the number of times this can happen?

Does it matter how wide the "spiral" is cut?

What would happen if the spiral were shorter or longer?

How does the amount of weight effect the amount of "stretch" in the spiral? Does twice the number of paper clips added to the spiral make it stretch twice as far?

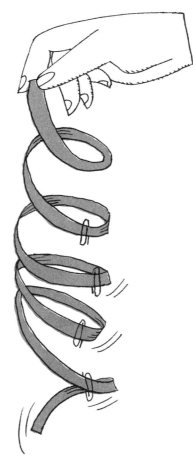

Does a straight piece of crepe paper stretch in the same way as a paper spiral stretches?

Is there a limit to how much weight may be added to a paper spiral if the spiral is to return to its original position?

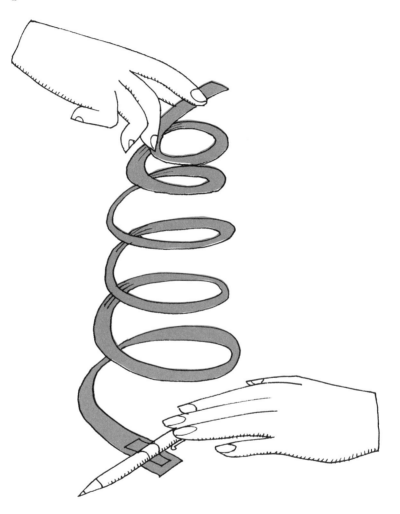

Is there a limit to how much weight may be added to the spiral without causing the spiral to break?

Sir Robert Hooke experimented with springs and observed many of the same things that you have just seen. He learned that the more weight is added to a stretchable object, the further the object stretches. Is there a limit to the "stretchability" of a rubber band?

Sir Robert Hooke took all of his observations and tried to fit all of the facts he collected into one general idea. He wanted this idea to be useful in describing and predicting what would happen to any object that could be stretched. The idea that he developed, we now call *Hooke's Law*. By carefully analyzing the information available from the experiments in this section, it is possible to recreate Hooke's Law. Try it! How does Hooke's Law apply to rubber bands?

Hooke also found that if too much weight is added to some stretchable materials, the material will not return to its original shape and size when the weight is removed. If this occurs, the object is said to have reached its *limit of elasticity*. Can the elastic limit be reached if rubber bands are used?

When weights are continuously added to any material, the material goes beyond its elastic limit and breaks. Because of this phenomenon, scientists, architects and engineers are very careful when deciding what materials to use when designing and making "things" for various purposes. What is the relationship between the "breaking point" and the tensile strength of a material?

GLOSSARY

ADHERE—to stick to an unlike substance.

ADHESION—the attractive force between unlike particles of matter.

AMBER—fossil resin from evergreen-type trees; may contain insects and other fossils; electrified by friction; a gem and ornamental mineral.

AMPLITUDE—the "strength" of a sound; usually refers to loudness.

BAROMETER—an instrument used to measure the pressure exerted by the atmosphere.

CAPILLARITY—the process of liquids moving in all directions through the small spaces between particles.

CAPILLARY ACTION—the rise or fall in the level of a liquid in a narrow tube; the action by which the surface of a liquid, where it is in contact with a solid, is raised or lowered.

COHERE—to stick to a like material; as an example, the particles of steel cohere to each other.

COHESION—the attractive force between like particles of matter.

COMPRESSIONAL STRENGTH—the resistance of a body to being pushed together, squeezed.

CONSERVATION OF MASS—refers to the idea that the amount of material of a substance does not change if the shape of the substance is altered.

CONSERVATION OF VOLUME—refers to the idea that the amount of space a substance takes up does not change when the shape is changed.

DA VINCI, LEONARDO (1452–1519)—Italian artist, scientist, inventor. He had a notion of inertia before Galileo understood that things acclerated as they fell; realized the impossibility of perpetual motion; studied the structure and function of the heart and valves and speculated on circulation a century before its discovery. Designed submarines and airplanes and invented the first elevator.

ELASTIC LIMIT—the amount of force applied to a stretchable substance that when exceeded will cause the substance to be deformed, i.e., it will not return to its original shape or size.

ENERGY—the ability to do work; energy is measured by the amount of work it can perform.

GALILEO (Galileo Galilei, 1564–1642)—one of the founders of modern science; made first useful astronomical telescope; discovered four large moons of Jupiter; investigated laws of motion of falling bodies.

GRAVITY—the force of attraction between any two objects. This force varies with the mass of the objects and their distances apart. Weight is a measurement of the gravitational attraction between a body and the earth.

HOOKE, ROBERT (1635–1703)—Englishman who built detailed compound microscope; proposed temperature scale with freezing point of water being 0°; invented a wheel barometer, seawater sampler, hygrometer, wind gage, rain gage, weathercock; worked on thermal expansion and formulated laws of elasticity.

INERTIA—the property that matter has of resisting changes in motion. A moving object does not come to rest, force is needed to change its motion, just as force is needed to start an object in motion.

MASS—the quantity of matter that a substance contains.

NEWTON, SIR ISAAC (1642–1727)—English mathematician, generally considered the greatest mathematician the world has yet produced; studied and discovered calculus, light and optics, laws of motion, laws of universal gravitation.

PITCH—the highness or lowness of a sound.

STATIC ELECTRICITY—electrical energy produced by friction that remains on/in the material as opposed to current, which is "electricity in motion."

TENSILE STRENGTH—the resistance of a body to being pulled apart.

TORRICELLI, EVANGELISTA (1608–1647)—Italian physicist and mathematician, studied with Galileo; he proposed the idea that we live in an ocean of air which exerts pressure on us. He devised an instrument, the mercury barometer, to measure this.

VIBRATIONS—in physics, the rapid back-and-forth movement of the particles that make up an elastic substance or material.

VOLUME—the amount of space a substance takes up.

YOUNG'S MODULUS—a constant value used in equations defining the behavior of elastic substances.

YOUNG, THOMAS (1773–1829)—Englishman who discovered interference of light waves, made first rough measurements of wavelengths of various colors; introduced present concept of energy; studied sound and elasticity (Young's Modulus); discovered astigmatism, explained accommodation (of eye) and developed theory of color vision.